Children of the World

Yugoslavia

For their help in the preparation of *Children of the World: Yugoslavia*, the editors gratefully thank: Employment and Immigration Canada, Ottawa, Ont.; the US Immigration and Naturalization Service, Washington DC; the Embassy of Yugoslavia (US), Washington, DC; the United States Department of State, Bureau of Public Affairs, Office of Public Communication, Washington, DC, for unencumbered use of material in the public domain; and V. Rev. Fr. M. P. Markovic, Pastor of the Saint Sava Serbian Orthodox Cathedral, Milwaukee, WI.

Library of Congress Cataloging-in-Publication Data

Yugoslavia / photography by Takako Yokotani.
    p. cm. — (Children of the world)
  "North American edition"—T.p. verso.
  Bibliography: p.
  Includes index.
  Summary: Presents the life of a nine-year-old-boy in a farming community in Yugoslavia, describing his family and the history, political system, and customs of his country.
  ISBN 1-555-32244-1. ISBN 1-555-32219-0 (lib. bdg.)
  1. Yugoslavia — Juvenile literature. 2. Children—Yugoslavia-
-Juvenile literature. [1. Yugoslavia—Social life and customs.
2. Family life—Yugoslavia.] I. Yokotani, Takako, ill.
II. Series: Children of the world (Milwaukee, Wis.)
DR1246.6.Y84 1988
949.7'024—dc 19   88-21053

North American edition first published in 1988 by

Gareth Stevens, Inc.
7317 West Green Tree Road
Milwaukee, Wisconsin 53223, USA

This work was originally published in shortened form consisting of section I only. Photographs and original text copyright © 1987 by Takako Yokotani. First and originally published by Kaisei-sha Publishing Co., Ltd., Tokyo. World English rights arranged with Kaisei-sha Publishing Co., Ltd. through Japan Foreign-Rights Centre.

Copyright this format © 1988 by Gareth Stevens, Inc.
Additional material and maps copyright © 1988 by Gareth Stevens, Inc.

Typeset by Zahn-Klicka-Hill, Milwaukee.
Map design: Sheri Gibbs.

1 2 3 4 5 6 7 8 9 93 92 91 90 89 88

Children of the World

Yugoslavia

Photography by
Takako Yokotani

Edited by
David K. Wright,
MaryLee Knowlton, &
Scott Enk

Gareth Stevens Publishing
Milwaukee

. . . a note about *Children of the World:*

The children of the world live in fishing towns, Arctic regions, and urban centers, on islands and in mountain valleys, on sheep ranches and fruit farms. This series follows one child in each country through the pattern of his or her life. Candid photographs show the children with their families, at school, at play, and in their communities. The text describes the dreams of the children and, often through their own words, tells how they see themselves and their lives.

Each book also explores events that are unique to the country in which the child lives, including festivals, religious ceremonies, and national holidays. The *Children of the World* series does more than tell about foreign countries. It introduces the children of each country and shows readers what it is like to be a child in that country.

. . . and about *Yugoslavia:*

Nine-year-old Pero and his family raise many vegetables and fruits, including olives and grapes. Pero lives in a small town on the Adriatic Coast. As the first son of a first son, he will inherit the family's 400-year-old farm when he grows up.

To enhance this book's value in libraries and classrooms, comprehensive reference sections include up-to-date data about Yugoslavia's geography, demographics, language, currency, education, culture, industry, and natural resources. *Yugoslavia* also features a bibliography, research topics, activity projects, and discussions of such subjects as Belgrade, the country's history, political system, ethnic and religious composition, and language.

The living conditions and experiences of children in Yugoslavia vary tremendously according to economic, environmental, and ethnic circumstances. The reference sections help bring to life for young readers the diversity and richness of the culture and heritage of Yugoslavia. Of particular interest are discussions of the cultures, political divisions, and national groups that have given Yugoslavia its multifaceted identity. Also of interest is the view this book offers of Yugoslavia as a member of both the European community at large and the Soviet-bloc nations of Eastern Europe.

CONTENTS

LIVING IN YUGOSLAVIA:
  Pero, a Young Farmer 6

Life in an Extended Family 10
A Large Working Family 14
Easter in Cilipi 20
A Day Trip to Dubrovnik 24
School Days 31
Summertime 41
A Summer Holiday in Cilipi 43
Yugoslavia — A Land of Many Histories 44

FOR YOUR INFORMATION: Yugoslavia 48

Official Name 48
Capital 48
History 48
Government 52
Currency 53
Education 53
Land and Climate 53
Map of Yugoslavia 54
Agriculture, Industry, and Natural Resources .. 56
Population and Ethnic Groups 56
Arts, Crafts, and Architecture 58
Sports and Recreation 59
Belgrade: The White City 60
Yugoslavs in North America 60
Glossary of Yugoslav Terms 61
More Books About Yugoslavia 61
Things to Do — Research 61
More Things to Do — Activities 62
Index 63

A family portrait includes many relatives: In back, Great-Uncle Miho, Cousin Eny, and Aunt Lucka. Middle row, Djuro, Grandmother, Grandfather, and Zorica. In front, sister Ana, brother Niko, Great-Grandmother, and Pero.

LIVING IN YUGOSLAVIA:
Pero, a Young Farmer

"Dobar dan!" says Pero Radovic. "Hello!" Pero is a nine-year-old boy from Cilipi, a village near the Adriatic Sea in Yugoslavia. Surrounded by cypress and olive trees, Cilipi hasn't changed much in the last 1,000 years. It hasn't grown much, either. Today it is home to around 800 people.

Pero's house has grown in 400 years! Today it has five bedrooms, two living rooms, a kitchen, a family room, and a covered porch.

Pero's house is in a cluster of other stone houses on the top of a hill. In his neighborhood, five other families are Radovics, too.

Mountains loom behind the village of Cilipi.

The Sunday meal needs more than one set of hands.

Setting the table is Pero's job on Sundays.

Life in an Extended Family

Pero lives in an extended family, a family made up of more than just one set of parents and their children. Pero's family is also close to relatives who don't live with them. The dinner table is always set for guests. On Sundays after church, all the relatives gather at Pero's house. The house, and the land that goes with it, is handed down to the oldest son of each generation. Some day, the house will belong to Pero. He will pass it on to his son.

The family enjoys the food and the company of a guest, Pero's uncle, who lives in Germany.

The Radovic women are good cooks. All three generations help prepare Sunday dinner. The meal today is soup, grilled chicken, homemade wine, goat cheese, and potatoes. Great-Grandmother made the cake for dessert. She has taught her daughter-in-law, who has taught her daughter-in-law, how to cook in the Radovic tradition, and everyone says she's still the family's best cook.

Dinner is delicious with fresh food well prepared.

House plants bloom in the sunroom.

The formal living room.

Pero's house has a large living room on each of its two floors.
The downstairs living room is used for meals and for relaxing.
Today, after Sunday dinner, family and friends gather around
the television to watch a show about a children's hospital in a
large city. Pero has never been to a large city, so he watches
the show carefully for glimpses of big-city life.

The upstairs living room is more formal. The family uses it for
baptisms and wedding receptions. Pictures of the family's
ancestors hang on the walls. The furniture, crystal, and linens
have been in the family for many generations and will be
preserved by generations to come.

Everyone gathers to relax in the family living room on the first floor.

The Radovics are Croatian. In Croatian families, the oldest son is given the name of his father's father. The oldest daughter is named after her father's mother. Since Pero's grandfather lives with him, everyone calls the younger Pero Perica, which means "little Pero."

When they are grown, younger sons must leave and start their own homes. Pero's Great-Uncle Miho left home at 18 to work in the United States. He and his family lived there for 12 years. Then they moved back to Yugoslavia, where they bought a big house with the money they had made in the United States. Uncle Miho tends his fields and lives a relaxed life.

Like many farmers in North America, Djuro has a job in town, too.

A Large Working Family

In Pero's family, everybody works. In his grandfather's day, farming was their only occupation. Now, in this area near the sea, the tourist industry provides many jobs. Many villagers work at the airport or in hotels and restaurants in the nearby tourist towns of Cavtat and Dubrovnik.

Pero's father has worked at the local airport for 20 years, since he was 14. He's part of the ground crew that repairs and checks the airplanes. He works two days and then takes a day off. On his days off, he's a farmer.

Pero's mother is a cook in a hotel in Cavtat. Today there is a buffet meal, so she's serving customers. She's glad to get out of the kitchen for a change and meet the people who eat there, especially the tourists, who come from all over the world. In modern times, women are expected to have jobs outside the home. In the cities, where grandparents might not live with their families, children are taken care of in government day care centers while their parents work.

Zorica has worked in Cavtat since she was a young girl.

Grandma Ana hangs clothes outside to dry.
Eight people make a lot of laundry!

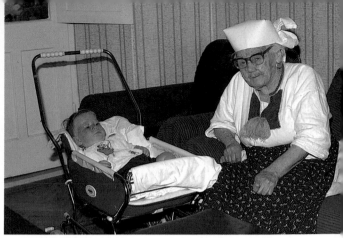

Great-Grandmother watches over baby Niko.

Homemade cheese.

Pero and his friends listen to Grandpa Pero.
During the day, he's in charge.

Pero's grandmother keeps the household running smoothly
during the week. She cooks, does laundry, makes cheese, and
looks after the children. In many rural areas and small towns
like Cilipi, the grandparents take care of the children while the
parents work. Pero enjoys his grandparents.

Pero and even little Ana help with the chores. Pero's daily job is
to deliver milk to his Uncle Miho's house. Uncle Miho pays him
for his work, but most of what Pero earns goes for textbooks
and school supplies.

15

For 400 years, Radovic men have worked this land.

Djuro inspects the grape crop.

Grandpa Pero is a full-time farmer, like his father before him and the generations of men before them. Perica wants to be a full-time farmer, too, and is learning from his grandfather. The two Peros are proud of their land and its products.

Summer and fall are dry and mild in Cilipi, perfect for growing grapes and olives. The Radovic family nurses its grapevines for three to four years until they bear fruit. They sell some of the grapes and use some to make their own wine.

Rebuilding the wall is hard work. But it should last another 400 years when it's done.

The whole family is involved in a big project — rebuilding a rock wall around the property. For two years now, they have been digging up rocks from the land and carrying them to the site of the wall. Younger brothers and sisters who have moved away come back to help keep the family land and buildings in good repair.

Olive farmers must be patient. The finest olives come from trees over 40 years old. In the old days, families planted an olive tree when each child was born, and the tree and child matured together.

The family also raises garden vegetables and fruits: four kinds of cabbage, beans, potatoes, lettuce, watermelons, pears, and peaches. Pero's family keeps cows, pigs, goats, and chickens in a pen in the backyard. Nearby is a smokehouse for curing meat. The Radovics, like other villagers, raise and preserve almost all their food.

Pero loves to ride his bike. Even today, villagers leave their doors unlocked.

Chickens poke around their backyard pen.

Homemade wine ages in casks in the cellar. Smoked hams line the back wall.

Aunt Lucka peels off the tough outer leaves of green vegetables.

Cheese ripens in a basket in the shade.

Raising this calf is Pero's job — not an easy one, he says.

The church stands high above the village.

Easter in Cilipi

On Good Friday, the Croatians in the village go to church. Women wear mourning clothes and men wear their best suits. They form a line behind a man carrying a crucifix and circle the church once before going inside. In the dim candlelight of the church, they mourn the death of Christ.

The villagers spend the days before Easter at home preparing for the holiday by baking bread and decorating eggs. Pero and Ana dye the eggs in rich colors to exchange with friends.

Easter comes at last. The whole village gathers at the church with cheerful faces. The women dress in traditional clothes to celebrate the Resurrection and the coming of spring. The majority of Yugoslavians are Serbs. As members of the Orthodox Church, they celebrate holidays at different times of the year.

On Good Friday, the villagers circle the church before entering.

Receiving Communion on Good Friday.

Good Friday services are very solemn.

At Easter Mass, the children's choir dresses in traditional clothing. Even their shoes match!

Two married women in traditional costume.

The square in front of the church, quiet during the week, is lively and colorful on Sundays. Easter Sunday is especially festive. After services, people gather to dance a traditional *kolo* of their region, Dalmatia. This dance is one of the most popular among all the many folk dances of Yugoslavia.

Sometimes foreign visitors come by bus from Cavtat or Dubrovnik to watch. Women in costume sell fine tablecloths and dolls. People joyfully greet each other and make plans to visit later in the day.

This Sunday, like all others, many of the women wear traditional costumes. Older women like Pero's grandmother and great-grandmother wear traditional clothes every day. In summer, they wear white cotton blouses, long skirts, and aprons. In winter, their blouses and skirts are wool.

Golden tassels and red braid adorn their blouses. Unmarried women wear small caps of red felt with golden braid. Married women wear large, starched white hats. Starching the wings of these wonderful hats takes practice.

Tourists can buy handmade crafts in the square.

22

Children sing in the square after Easter Mass.

Easter bread and eggs make a lovely, bright table.

Children are important to the church service, helping the priests and singing.

23

At one time, Dubrovnik was a great trading port. Today it is a tourist attraction. The brilliant blue Adriatic Sea serves both traders and tourists.

A Day Trip to Dubrovnik

About 16 miles (26 km) north of Cilipi is the "Pearl of the Adriatic Sea," Dubrovnik. All along the Adriatic coast are remains of ancient Roman cities that grew and prospered about 2,000 years ago. The city of Dubrovnik was founded about 1,300 years ago on the site of an old Roman town. Once it was a port and center of trade. Today, it is one of Europe's most famous tourist spots. In its old section you can still see a fountain from the 1400s, a magnificent stone church, and an old monastery. From the castle wall that surrounds the old city, you can see the red tiled roofs of ancient homes. Stone streets lined with cafés and seafood restaurants wind their way to the wall.

Though he lives less than an hour away, Pero has rarely been to Dubrovnik. So today's trip with his parents and his sister is a real treat. He has brought some of the money he makes delivering milk to his uncle. He plans to buy something that will always remind him of this day.

24

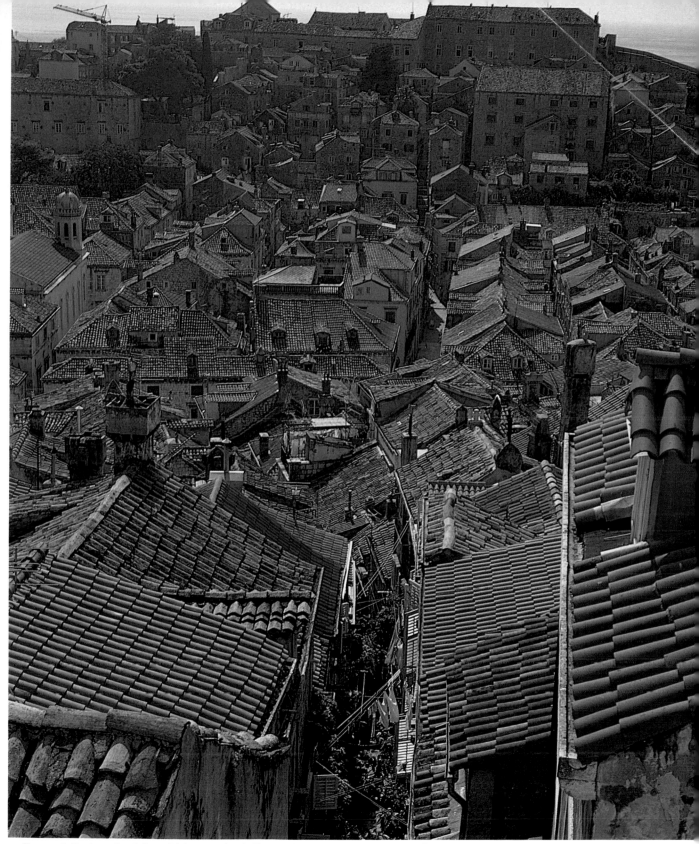

The red tiled roofs of the old houses look like roofs in countries all along the Adriatic coastline.

The Placa in the old section of Dubrovnik.

Just inside the gates to the old city is the Placa, which is pronounced "plaht-za." The Placa is a broad street that leads straight through the city from one gate to the other. Here visitors once had to wash themselves in the fountain before they could enter the city. Even today the Placa is closed to cars and buses. But it's not a quiet street. It's usually crowded with tourists. Getting lost in Dubrovnik is impossible because all streets lead to the Placa.

Pero and his family feel like tourists in Dubrovnik. They stroll along the Placa, window-shopping. They pass stores selling clothes, shoes, stationery, gifts, and other items that attract tourists. Pero especially loves the toys and brightly colored tablets and notebooks.

The streets of Dubrovnik. Great stone buildings and narrow stairways lead up to the castle wall.

The city of Dubrovnik has a motto — *Libertas*. It means "liberty" and it says a lot about the history of this special city. For hundred of years outsiders ruled cities all along the Adriatic. Only Dubrovnik remained an independent city-state.

As a city-state, Dubrovnik managed its own affairs. It survived a fire in the 1200s, a plague in the 1500s, and an earthquake and tidal wave in the 1600s. The wealth it gained from trading allowed it to pay for protection from invaders who wanted to rule it from Spain, Turkey, and Rome. The independence brought by these payoffs allowed the leaders to develop their society. In the 1400s alone, Dubrovnik outlawed the slave trade, provided public heath care, built a water supply system under the roads, and began a free education program. The rest of the world did not become this civilized until hundreds of years later.

Visitors circle the old city by walking
along the top of the wall.

The ancient walls that surround the old city of Dubrovnik are thick. They remind visitors that it took more than money to preserve the independence of the city-state. Pero and his family climb its steep steps to walk around the old city. Most of the wall is still intact after nearly 1,000 years, and the Yugoslavian government is restoring what has crumbled. The children tire long before their walk is over. They talk their parents into getting a pizza. Pizza came to Dubrovnik with the tourists. These children from Cilipi have never had it before.

Tourist boats provide tours of the harbor.

The flagstones of the alleys are worn smooth by centuries of walking feet.

Pero and his family visit the Pijaca, a market in the square behind the church. They feel at home here, because this Pijaca is just like theirs at home and in most other Yugoslavian towns, only bigger. Here merchants cater to the tourists as well as the townspeople. They sell fruits, vegetables, and whatever else they can get the tourists to buy. In the houses above and around the market, daily life goes on — laundry stretches high across alleys and between windows.

Just as the family leaves the Pijaca, Pero finds what he wants to buy with the money in his pocket. In a small shop just off the square, he sees a picture of children dancing the kolo. He buys it as a souvenir of his trip to Dubrovnik.

The Pijaca offers fresh fruits and vegetables from spring through autumn.

Bookshops and art galleries are tucked into back alleys.

Not yet! Please, not yet!

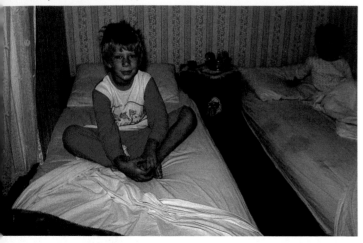

Shirt . . .

Teeth . . .

Shoes . . .

Breakfast . . .

And he's off!

The three friends set out.

School Days

Pero rolls over and groans when his mother wakes him. Getting up for school is hard enough, but today, it's harder, because it's the first day of Daylight Saving Time. Wake-up time has come an hour earlier. His clothes for the day are folded at the foot of his bed, so he dresses, brushes his teeth, and heads downstairs for breakfast.

Pero and Zorica are the first ones to leave the house in the morning. They enjoy a quiet breakfast together each day. Bread, jam, and cocoa are a pleasant way to start a busy day. By 7:30 they're both out the door. Waiting to walk to school with Pero are his friends Mato and Nikolina. If they don't poke around too much, the walk takes about 20 minutes.

Pero and his schoolmates. Their school is for children in the first through fourth grades.

Because Cilipi is so small, its school is only for children in the first through fourth grades. Older children are bused to a school in the nearby town of Cavtat. Pero is in the third grade. His school has just two classrooms for 62 students. First and second graders are in one class, and third and fourth graders are in the other. Classes are held every day but Sunday from 8:00 till noon.

Students arrive at the school a little before 8:00. Some come earlier to play before classes start. By the time Pero gets there, many of his friends are already gathered around the door, teasing and chasing each other. When the teacher gives a signal, they form four lines and file quietly into the building, first graders first. The day has begun.

33

Pero's first class is Croatian. Yugoslavia has many dialects and three official languages. Cilipi is in Croatia, so Pero and his friends study Croatian. Yugoslavia's other main language is Serbian, which sounds like Croatian but looks different because it uses a different alphabet. Usually the two languages are grouped together in one language called Serbo-Croatian.

Math class. The first question is easy.

Pero also takes math, social studies, drawing, physical education, and music. English classes begin in third grade. The children come to school an hour early on Mondays and Tuesdays to learn English. School clubs meet after classes. Children can learn about painting, guitar, drama, photography, and other things depending on their interests and their teacher's abilities. The school only has two teachers, so what they teach depends on what they know or can do.

The teacher passes out the answer sheets for an English test.

Winning pictures from a contest hang in the hall.

Four classes meet each day. After the second class there is a half-hour recess. The children dash for the door. Out on the playground, they gather in groups and open small bundles they've brought from home. What's the snack today? Most of the children have sandwiches and cake and brightly colored eggs left over from Easter. Pero has some Easter bread, carefully wrapped so it doesn't crumble.

From noon to 1:00 on Fridays, children meet for Pioneer Organization. This is a class for communist education. The students hear stories about the Yugoslav heroes of World War II and their fight against the fascists of Germany and its allies. They also learn the socialist ideals of Yugoslavia's government.

Recess is everybody's favorite time!

After a snack, the children stay active in physical education class.

A lively game of high-jump shows who's agile.

School's out!

Walking home through the woods.

Most days, this donkey comes out to meet the children.
Sometimes they give him leftovers from their snacks.

36

Pero and his mother are learning English together, Pero from books and Zorica from tourists at the hotel.

After school, Pero and his friends walk home through the cypress trees. Sometimes they explore the forest or climb trees, so it takes a little longer to get home than it did to get to school. Only one street they cross has cars. The rest of the way is a quiet village path where they're more likely to meet a donkey than a car.

Zorica gets home about the same time as Pero, after she cooks the noon meal at the hotel. Pero sits at the dining room table to do his homework before he's off to do his chores. His mother helps him before she does her housework.

Pero's school books.

Walking home through the woods.

Pero pilots the boat across the smooth water.

Something had better bite soon. Pero tries to
catch his supper.

A quick swim before supper.

A stone beach is rough. Children learn to swim so they don't have to stand in the water.

Summertime

It's vacation! All along the Adriatic coast, beaches and campsites fill with visitors. Yugoslavians and foreigners come in cars packed with camping gear to stay for a few days or a few weeks.

Early in the summer, Pero's parents take the children to Cavtat to swim and fish. By the end of the summer, the beaches will be crowded and polluted, but for now, the water is clear. Pero and his father take a boat to the campsite where Djuro is spending his vacation. They call their campsite the "Men's House."

41

Pero eats melon from home while the fish are frying.

The men show off their catch before cooking it.

Everybody is hungry.

The men sleep on cots under a canopy.

The men of the village spend their vacations at their campsite. Women and children can visit during the day, but they must leave after dinner. Women do not have vacations like this.

Djuro is on vacation all week. He and Pero have brought water and groceries to the campsite by boat. After a day of fishing and swimming, they are very hungry. They clean, fry, and eat the fish they've caught. As the sun sets, the men light a lantern and Pero gets ready to go home. He can't wait until he is old enough to stay all night.

Children learn early to honor their ancestors.

A Summer Holiday in Cilipi

The last Sunday of July is a village holiday. Everyone goes to the cemetery outside town to visit family graves. They hold a service there today, honoring their ancestors. After the service, family members put flowers on the graves. Flowers completely cover the older graves because many of the villagers trace their families back to the same people.

The traditions of Cilipi are old and strongly rooted. But with each generation, there are some changes. Pero is the first in his family to learn English in school. His world will be a little bigger than his father's.

Yugoslavia — A Land of Many Histories

Yugoslavia is a country with six republics, five large ethnic groups, many small ones, four major languages, three major religions, and two alphabets. The people have a wide range of beliefs and histories. Yet since 1946, they have been one country. The government of Yugoslavia has encouraged people to preserve their traditions.

The old traditions give people a sense of history. Through these customs people trace a history separate from the Yugoslav government — a history of families, traditions, and beliefs. If you look closely, you can sometimes see history in the traditional costumes of the people.

Bosnia-Hercegovina

The effects of over 400 years of Turkish occupation are clearly seen in Bosnia-Hercegovina. You can still eat Turkish foods and hear young girls singing *sevdalinka* — old Turkish songs of lost love. Bosnia-Hercegovina's capital city, Sarajevo, was the site of the 1984 Winter Olympic Games. But Sarajevo was world-famous before then: Here a student named Gavrilo Princip assassinated the heir to the Austrian throne. His act started World War I.

The people today gathered under the name of the Republic of Croatia have thought of themselves as Croats for a thousand years. Politically, though, they have been controlled by nearly every other ruler in the region at some time. The customs and costumes of the region show the influence that foreign rule has had on the people. Some women wear a kerchief in the Venetian style. Others wear a small cap. Men's outfits often have Turkish-type pants. Some men also wear a cap that looks like a turban. Women's dresses can be either dark wool or white linen, but they are always embroidered with beautiful designs in red or gold.

Croatia

Vojvodina

Vojvodina is a province within the Serbian republic. Here, in the rich, rolling hills, the farmers grow enough food to feed the whole country. Amid the fields of wheat, corn, and sunflowers is Yugoslavia's most varied population — Hungarian, Slovakian, Ruthenian, and Romanian. The schools of Vojvodina teach children in their ethnic languages to preserve their culture.

Macedonia has been pulled back, forth, and sideways through the centuries by Albania, Yugoslavia, Bulgaria, Greece, and Turkey. It wasn't until after World War II that the Macedonian language could be legally and safely spoken for the first time in centuries. In Skopje, its capital city, the ancient and modern meet. The new city was built with world aid after a terrible earthquake in 1963 killed 1,100 people and left over 100,000 homeless. In the modern part of the city, kids in fashionable clothes watch VCRs and listen to stereos. If you cross the Kameni Most, an old bridge that divides the city, you come to the old city. Here you find the Islamic community with its Oriental bazaars and buildings.

Macedonia

Serbia

Serbia is the largest of the republics. It has Yugoslavia's capital city, Belgrade, which means "white city." Actually Belgrade is a gray city which grew from a well-placed fort into a major city. From the fort, then called Kalemegdan, warriors fought off invaders where the Danube and Sava rivers meet. It was lost often to many peoples, including Romans, Huns, Avars, Hungarians, Turks, and finally, Germans who came by air rather than by water.

46

Montenegro, which means "black mountain," is the smallest of the republics, known for its rugged mountains and harsh weather. Throughout the centuries, the men of Montenegro have been known as fierce warriors. Using the mountains to hide in, they fought the Turks for hundreds of years. In World War II, they used the same tactics to fight the Italians who had been sent by the Germans to occupy their land. The man's costume is a fancy version of a military uniform.

Montenegro

Slovenia is the most European of the Yugoslavian republics. It was once part of the Austro-Hungarian Empire and was not ruled by Turks, as much of the rest of the country was. Its traditional clothes are like the costumes of Austria, with short jackets and leather shorts for men. Women wear full skirts with a cap or scarf and a belt with ribbons hanging from it. In the tiny town of Lipica, the famous Lippizaner horses were first raised. They have been bred here since 1580.

Slovenia

47

FOR YOUR INFORMATION:
Yugoslavia

Official Name: Socijalistička Federativna Republika Jugoslavija
(SOHTS-ee-ah-lees-teech-kah FEH-deh-rah-teev-nah
REH-poo-blee-kah YOO-go-slah-vee-yah)
Socialist Federal Republic of Yugoslavia

Capital: Belgrade

History

Yugoslavia is not what we would call a melting-pot nation. Dozens of different ethnic groups have lived side by side there for centuries, but commonly they do not intermarry or worship together or even fight on the same side in a war. The history of the country explains why this might be so.

Buildings from the 19th and 20th centuries share a view of the river.

Yugoslavia's First Residents

The first visitors to what is now Yugoslavia may have been the Greeks. They built settlements all along the Adriatic coast, beginning in about 600 BC. At that time, the area was called Illyria.

The Greeks were followed by the Romans, who passed through Yugoslavia on their way to conquering other lands. After the Romans conquered Illyria in 167 BC, they divided it into four provinces, or districts: Illyricum, Dalmatia, Moesia, and Pannonia. Romans settled mostly in the western half of the country, and people from what is now Turkey settled in the east.

The first people called Slavs came from the north in about AD 600. For almost 1,000 years, they battled Germans, Turks, Bulgarians, Austrians, and Italians. Beginning in the 9th century, Greek missionaries, Italian monks, and others introduced the Slavs to Christianity. Two famous Greek missionaries, Cyril and Methodius, have been called "Apostles to the Slavs." According to tradition, Cyril invented an alphabet used even today by many Yugoslavs. We call it the Cyrillic alphabet.

By the 10th century, one group of Slavs, the Croats, had established their own kingdom in what is now northwest Yugoslavia. In 1089, their kingdom was combined with Hungary. During the following centuries, Hungary would gain more control over Croatia.

Another Slavic people, the Serbs, were to the east of the Croats. They'd begun settling in the 7th century. By the 14th century, the Serbs, under King Stephen Dušan, had built one of the most powerful kingdoms in eastern Europe. After this king died, Serbia fell to the Turks. They would rule it for some 500 years.

As a result, until the 19th century, much of what is now Yugoslavia was under the control of either Austria or Turkey or the Italian city of Venice. But the Croats, Serbs, and other peoples living in the conquered lands did not adopt the ways of their conquerors. They all looked to the day when they would gain freedom from foreign rule.

During the 18th and 19th centuries, Austria's Habsburg empire was able to control unrest in its portion of Yugoslavia, but Turkey's hold on its share of Yugoslavia got weaker and weaker. In 1878, Serbia and Montenegro gained independence from Turkey. In that same year, troops from the new Austro-Hungarian empire invaded Bosnia-Hercegovina. In 1908, Austria-Hungary made this land part of its own territory.

In 1912, Serbia and Montenegro joined Bulgaria and Greece in a war against Turkey. When the war ended the next year, Macedonia and much of what is now southern Yugoslavia had also gained freedom from Turkish rule.

Independence — and War

For a few exciting years, Serbia and Montenegro were truly independent. But, by this time, many Croats, Slovenes, and Serbs were concerned with breaking free from the power of Austria-Hungary. In 1914, a Serbian named Gavrilo Princip, seeking freedom from Austria-Hungary, shot Archduke Francis Ferdinand, heir to the Austrian throne. This dramatic event, which took place in the city of Sarajevo, was the spark that started World War I.

After four and half years of brutal fighting all over Europe, Austria-Hungary and Germany lost the world's first Great War, as it was then called. One result was that the Kingdom of the Serbs, Croats, and Slovenes was formed on December 1, 1918. King Peter I of Serbia ruled the new country.

But unrest continued because many Croations wanted independence from Yugoslavia. This caused friction among the country's different groups. In 1928, after much heated debate in parliament, a Montenegrin member of parliament shot and killed a Croatian member and two of his supporters. Angered by this, Croation leaders declared their area was no longer going to be part of the kingdom.

It seemed that the whole country was about to plunge into civil war. King Peter's son and successor, Alexander I, tried to stop the unrest by taking dictatorial control of the government. He tried to convince the people that they were all part of one country, rather than members of different groups. To emphasize unity, in 1929, he gave the Kingdom of the Serbs, Croats, and Slovenes a new name: Yugoslavia, or the Land of the South Slavs.

In 1934, an unhappy Macedonian assassinated King Alexander I. Clearly, getting everyone to work together was proving to be difficult in this nation.

The Nazis Invade

Yugoslavia's troubles continued. In the 1930s, German dictator Adolf Hitler built his country into a frightening and brutal military machine. Hitler's goal was to conquer Europe and then the world. Prince Regent Paul, who now ruled, signed a friendship agreement with the Germans in 1941. Later that year, Nazi Germany and Italy invaded Yugoslavia and overthrew the government. Two major guerrilla armies formed. From 1941 to 1945, these armies attacked German troops and resisted Nazi rule. Sometimes they attacked each other.

Many people living in Yugoslavia did not live to see the end of World War II. Gypsies, Jews, communists, guerrilla soldiers, and anyone who tried to help members of these groups were killed by the Nazis. Throughout Europe, millions of people died at the hands of the Nazis.

Some people in Yugoslavia agreed with Nazi goals. Some Croatians were pro-German or pro-Austrian. They spied on people they thought were anti-German. To punish and frighten people, the Nazis sent entire villages to slave labor camps. Many Yugoslavs were shot or gassed to death.

But many other groups in Yugoslavia supported the guerrillas. They helped push the Nazis out of the country by 1945.

Tito: A Yugoslavian Communist

One guerrilla group was led by a Croatian named Josip Broz Tito. Tito was born in 1892 into a large, poor peasant family. When he was 13 years old, he began studying to be a locksmith. Later, he became a metalworker. During this time, he became involved in socialist politics. Because government officials didn't like his political ideas, they sometimes had him arrested and jailed. In 1927, he became the leader of the Communist Party in Zagreb.

From then until the beginning of World War II, Tito rose in the eyes of world communism. He organized youth groups, workers' groups, and farmers. He attended International Communist Party meetings, often by sneaking in and out of Yugoslavia. In 1928, Tito was again arrested. He was sentenced to five years in prison. His activities had yet another price — his two children died because of ill health and poverty.

During World War II, Tito and his followers fought from hideouts in Yugoslavia's rugged mountains. By 1943, Tito's Partisans, as they were called, had 250,000 members and had established a government. The other group of guerrillas supported the idea of having a kingdom again after the war. But Tito and other communists declared themselves the heads of a new government in March 1945. Later that year, Tito won a national election, but his government had banned many opposing political groups from running candidates.

Many people believed Tito would be just another dictator under the thumb of the Soviet Union. His government took over many stores and factories, took away workers' rights, restricted religious freedom and free speech, and silenced newspapers and people who opposed him. But he surprised the world when, in 1948, he refused to let the Soviets control his country. This decision helped Yugoslavia immensely, since the people could then develop trade relations and other ties with both communist and non-communist countries. Tito always insisted that Yugoslavia had the right to decide for itself how it would build a communist society.

Tito died in May 1980, just before he would have turned 88. Since then, Yugoslavia has continued to follow a communist path that often differs from the path taken in the Soviet Union. There are some limited freedoms, mostly in the areas of the arts, travel, and small business. In fact, some Yugoslav businesses are now privately owned. But freedom of speech and expression is still restricted, especially when it comes to criticizing the government.

Government

Yugoslavia calls itself a "socialist federal republic." It is a communist nation made up of six states, which are also called republics. The six states are Croatia, Slovenia, Bosnia-Hercegovina, Macedonia, Montenegro, and Serbia, which includes the provinces of Vojvodina and Kosovo. The country is run by a nine-member council called the Presidency, a two-house lawmaking body called the Federal Assembly, and a cabinet called the Federal Executive Council. The head of the Federal Executive Council, called the premier, is the head of Yugoslavia's government.

The members of the Federal Assembly are elected. But the only legal political party presenting candidates is the League of Communists of Yugoslavia, so voters do not have the choices they have in more democratic nations.

The government operates under a constitution created in 1974. Yugoslavs call their government socialist self-management. This means that the government runs the country, but that individual people are also responsible for the future of their society. Citizens are free to try to improve the quality of their lives in any legal way, but they cannot make protests against government officials or policies. The government controls national radio, television, and news outlets.

According to Yugoslav law, all citizens have the right to health care, the vote, and self-betterment. They also may join political organizations — if the League of Communists of Yugoslavia approves of them. Yugoslavia's government and social system have given the country the best standard of living it has ever seen. Still, many Yugoslavs work in other European countries where wages are higher.

Yugoslavia has good relations with all its neighbors except Albania. Albania has been accused by Yugoslavia of stirring up trouble among Yugoslavs of Albanian heritage, but Albania's government has claimed that Yugoslavia has mistreated people of Albanian heritage living in Kosovo. Being a communist country but not part of the Soviet bloc allows Yugoslavia to criticize the Soviet Union as it sees fit.

Banners of political leaders adorn buildings.

Currency

Yugoslavia's unit of currency is the *dinar*. Currently it takes about 500 dinar to equal one United States dollar.

Education

Yugoslav children attend elementary school for eight years, from ages 7 through 14. They are taught history, mathematics, science, geography, art, and physical education. From there, students can go on to a vocational school or a high school. Some take on-the-job training. Few students attend college, but good students are free to attend colleges in or outside their native land.

Despite intense efforts by the government to improve the school system, about 10 to 15 percent of Yugoslavs over 10 years of age still cannot read. The country's many languages and ethnic groups make it difficult to raise Yugoslavia's literacy rate.

Land and Climate

Yugoslavia is about the size of Wyoming. The country's total area is 98,766 square miles (255,804 sq km). It has seven neighbors. Starting in the northwest and traveling clockwise, the neighboring countries are Italy, Austria, Hungary, Romania, Bulgaria, Greece, and Albania.

Three very different areas are present in Yugoslavia. Each has its own climate. The most famous is the warm west coast, with 220 days of sunshine each year. East of the Adriatic seacoast are rows of mountains that run across half the country. The highest mountains, called the Julian Alps, reach 9,393 feet (2,863 m) in the northwest. The northeast has vast fertile plains around the Danube River.

The most prosperous parts of Yugoslavia are near the coast, which is more than 375 miles (600 km) long. Tourists from all over the world come to enjoy clean water, warm weather, and beautiful little towns and harbors. The center of the country has become a winter recreation area. Sarajevo, about halfway between the capital of Belgrade and the coast, was the site of the 1984 Winter Olympics. It is easily reached by Europeans and Turks alike, so its culture combines the two traditions. Much of southern Yugoslavia is rocky, dry, and poor.

Yugoslavia is dotted with more than 300 lakes. There are 1,850 rivers at least six miles (10 km) long. About one-third of the country is covered with forest. More than half of the country is considered farmland. Temperatures range from far below freezing atop the mountains in winter to 90°F (32°C) or more along the coast and on the northeast plain in the summer.

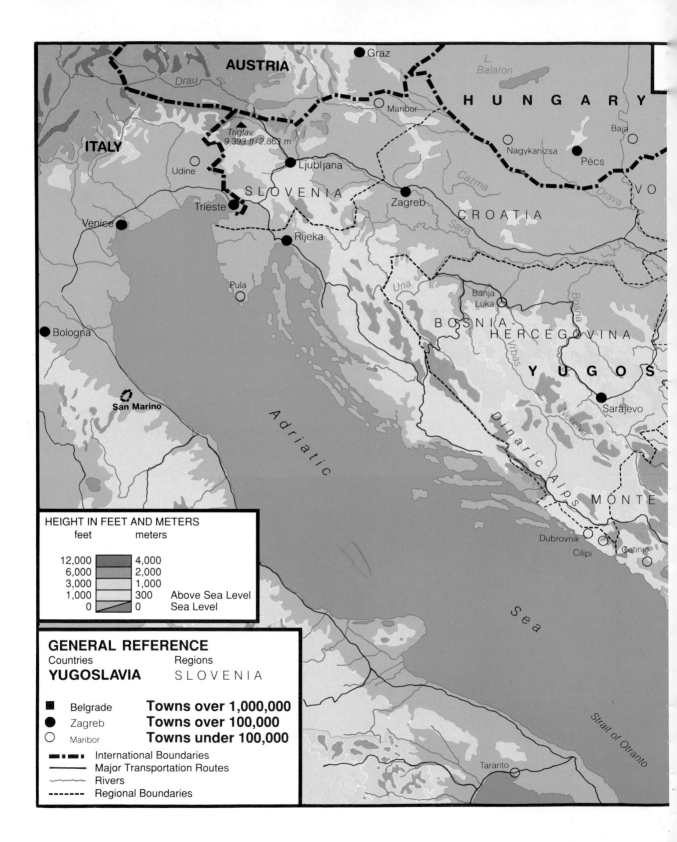

AUSTRIA

● Graz

Drau

ITALY

L. Balaton

H U N G A R Y

○ Maribor

Baja ○

Triglav
9,393 ft / 2,863 m

Nagykanizsa ○

Pécs ●

Udine ○

Ljubljana ●

S L O V E N I A

Cazma

● Zagreb

Drava

V O

C R O A T I A

Sava

Trieste ●

Venice ●

Rijeka ●

Una

Banja
Luka ○

B O S N I A -

Vrbas

Bosna

Pula ○

H E R C E G O V I N A

Y U G O S

Bologna ●

A d r i a t i c

Neretva

● Sarajevo

San Marino

Dinaric Alps

M O N T E

Dubrovnik ○
Cilipi

○ Cetinje

S e a

Strait of Otranto

Taranto ○

HEIGHT IN FEET AND METERS

feet	meters	
12,000	4,000	
6,000	2,000	
3,000	1,000	
1,000	300	Above Sea Level
0	0	Sea Level

GENERAL REFERENCE

Countries   Regions
YUGOSLAVIA   SLOVENIA

■ Belgrade   **Towns over 1,000,000**
● Zagreb   **Towns over 100,000**
○ Maribor   **Towns under 100,000**
▄▬▪▬▪ International Boundaries
─── Major Transportation Routes
─── Rivers
----- Regional Boundaries

YUGOSLAVIA — Political and Physical

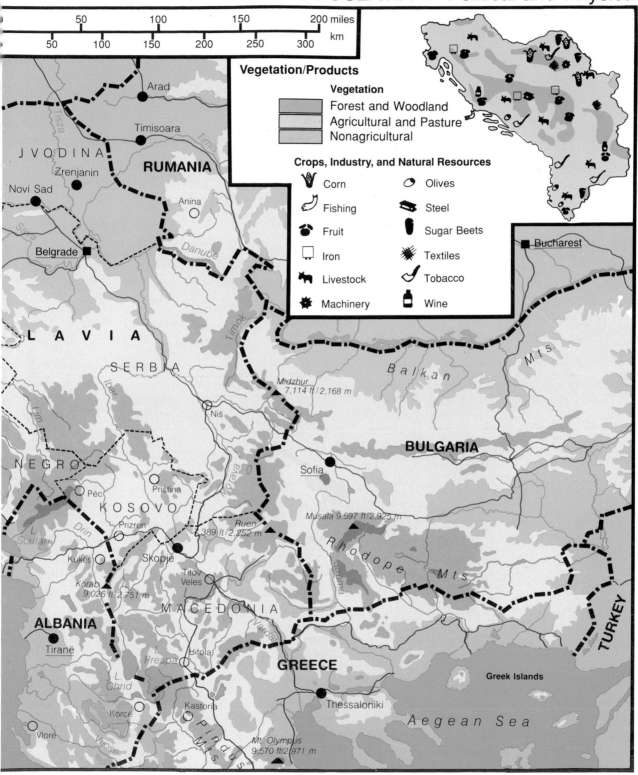

Vegetation/Products

Vegetation
Forest and Woodland
Agricultural and Pasture
Nonagricultural

Crops, Industry, and Natural Resources

Corn
Fishing
Fruit
Iron
Livestock
Machinery

Olives
Steel
Sugar Beets
Textiles
Tobacco
Wine

50   100   150   200 miles
50 100 150 200 250 300 km

Arad

Timisoara

J V O D I N A

RUMANIA

Zrenjanin

Novi Sad

Anina

Sava

Belgrade

Danube

L A V I A

SERBIA

Tisza

Timis

Timok

Midzhur
7,114 ft / 2,168 m

Niš

Bucharest

Balkan   Mts.

BULGARIA

Sofia

Ibar

Lim

N E G R O

Pristina

Péc

K O S O V O

Morava

Prizren

Ruen
7,389 ft / 2,252 m

Musala 9,597 ft / 2,925 m

Drin

L.
Scutari

Kukés

Skopje

Titov
Veles

R h o d o p e   Mts.

Struma

Korab
9,026 ft / 2,751 m

M A C E D O N I A

ALBANIA

Tiranë

L.
Prespa

Bitola

Vardar

GREECE

TURKEY

L.
Ohrid

Korçë

Kastoria

Thessaloniki

Greek Islands

Vlorë

P i n d u s   Mts.

Vjose

Mt. Olympus
9,570 ft / 2,971 m

A e g e a n   S e a

Agriculture, Industry, and Natural Resources

Fewer farmers are producing more goods in Yugoslavia these days. That is because there are more tractors, better seeds, more fertilizer, and better breeds of livestock than in the past. Farmers made up more than three-quarters of the population before World War II. Today, fewer Yugoslavs — under 30 percent — live on farms. Farmers produce wheat, corn, sugar beets, beef, pork, or lamb.

But where did the other farmers go? Fortunately, industrial development has absorbed many of these workers. Yugoslavia is a developing country. That means its factories are new — or still on the drawing boards. It also means that wages are low but slowly climbing. Yugoslavia is a leading producer of wood products, processed food, machinery, leather goods, and textiles. The average income of a Yugoslav is $3,109 a year.

Tourism is big business in the country. Originally, incredibly beautiful villages and natural wonders lured vacationers to Yugoslavia. The government responded by developing modern hotels and related facilities. Many people from poorer parts of the country work part of the year in the scenic area known as the Dalmatian Coast. In the 1980s, tourism brought an average of more than $1 billion into the country each year.

Population and Ethnic Groups

There were about 23.5 million Yugoslavs as of mid-1988. Not all of them live in Yugoslavia. As many as 1.5 million, mostly men, work in Europe or in North America. Most return home to invest their savings in a farm or a home.

Most people don't think of themselves as Yugoslavs. Instead, they identify with a particular region. There are approximately 8.5 million Serbs, 4.7 million Croats, 2.1 million Bosnian Muslims, 1.9 million Slovenes, 1.9 million Albanians, and 1.4 million Macedonians. There are many more minorities. They include Montenegrins, Hungarians, Turks, Slovaks, Romanians, Bulgarians, Ruthenes, Czechs, Italians, Russians, and Ukrainians, among others.

Such variety can be good and bad. Different ethnic groups sometimes don't get along with each other. At the moment, some persons of Albanian heritage are especially upset. Most of them live in Kosovo, which is controlled by Serbia. They insist on complete self-government and their own language. The country is a hodgepodge of people who don't really trust each other.

For each ethnic group, there seems to be a unique language. The two largest groups, the Serbs and the Croats, speak the same language. Most Muslims and Montenegrins also speak Serbo-Croatian. To complicate things, there are two alphabets. One is Latin and is similar to the English alphabet. The

other, Cyrillic, is a lot like the Russian alphabet. A traveler crossing
the country could easily find a different language in every major town.

Neighboring Albania boasts that it is the world's first atheist state. Most
Yugoslavs, however, are deeply religious. Religion is practiced, even though
Yugoslavia is a communist state. More than 40% of all Yugoslavs are members
of Eastern Orthodox churches, about 30% are Roman Catholics, and 12% Muslims.

Yugoslavia's communist government helps preserve the country's old and
beautiful religious art and architecture, which attracts tourists. It will even
promote religious activity if it brings tourists with money to spend. In 1981,
six Yugoslav children said they had a religious vision near the small town
of Medjugorje. Christians began to visit the site where the children reported
seeing the Virgin Mary every evening. At first, the government discouraged
people from joining the children, but now the government-owned airline brings
Christians each week from eight major cities in the United States to witness the
daily event. Officially, however, the government favors atheism.

The Major Groups

Yugoslavia means "Land of the Southern Slavs." Does that mean all Yugoslavs
are alike and different from northern Slavs? They aren't. There are three
official languages — Serbo-Croatian, Slovenian, and Macedonian — and three
major religions — Eastern Orthodoxy, Roman Catholicism, and Islam. On top of
this, Yugoslavia has six separate republics with several different ethnic groups.
Here is a look at each republic:

• Serbia is the largest republic, both in size and population. It is also the most
troubled. Serbs and Albanians disagree over who should run Kosovo, or
southern Serbia. Yugoslavia's capital, Belgrade, is in the northern half of
Serbia. Belgrade has more than 1.4 million residents, making it Yugoslavia's
largest city. The Serbian countryside is hilly and wooded. The best farmland
is in the north near the Danube River.

• Croatia is second only to Serbia in population. Serbs and Croats use
different alphabets, but speak the same language, Serbo-Croatian. Croatia
takes in almost all of the Dalmatian Coast, where tourists visit in great numbers.
The capital of Croatia is the ancient city of Zagreb, the second largest city in
Yugoslavia. Other important places are Split, a city on the coast that dates
back to ancient Roman times but has many modern buildings, and Dubrovnik,
a seaport and tourist attraction.

• Bosnia-Hercegovina, between Serbia and Croatia, was the site of the 1984
Winter Olympics. They were held in the capital of the republic, Sarajevo,
located in a valley in the Dinaric Alps. The republic is mountainous, and warm
enough in places to grow grapes and plums for wine and other beverages,

including *šljivovicu,* a plum brandy that is Yugoslavia's national drink. In the colder mountain areas, winter sports attract a growing number of visitors.

• Slovenia is Yugoslavia's northernmost republic. It has snow-capped peaks that are part of the Julian Alps. Its capital and largest city is Ljubljana, a mixture of modern and medieval architecture — including a fort and a cathedral. The republic features dramatic scenery similar to that in Switzerland or northern Italy. But Slovenia is also Yugoslavia's most heavily industrialized republic. Its manufacturing and mining industries also make it the wealthiest.

• Macedonia is warm and dry. This republic was once part of, and is named after, a great kingdom of ancient Greece ruled by Alexander the Great. Greek influence is still strong here. But many other ethnic groups — including Bulgarians, Slavs, Albanians, Turks, and a rural people called the Vlach — now live in this republic. Eastern Orthodox churches dot the landscape. The border here between Yugoslavia and Albania has several scenic and appealing lakes filled with freshwater fish. In 1963, more than 1,000 persons died in the capital, Skopje, as the result of an earthquake.

• Montenegro is between Bosnia-Hercegovina and Serbia on the Dalmation Coast. Its largest city, Titograd, is an industrial center. Until the city was renamed in 1946, it was called Podgorica. Titograd still has a few buildings that show its Turkish heritage, including a tower and a mosque. The ocean water here is said to be the cleanest in Europe. Italy is just a ferry-boat ride west of the resort village of Bar.

Arts, Crafts, and Architecture

Visitors expecting to see Yugoslavs in quaint costumes are in for a big surprise. Modern-day residents wear jeans and tennis shoes or other clothing we think of as fashionable. But that does not mean native costumes have disappeared. These ancient, colorful outfits are put on for holidays or seen at times in rural areas. A trained eye can look at a Yugoslav in his or her ethnic dress and identify the wearer's heritage, language, and religion.

Yugoslavia's architecture also reflects its religious history. All across the country, ancient churches contain religious paintings and statues hundreds of years old. Mixing traditions of eastern and western Christianity, the paintings depict Biblical scenes or tell of the lives of saints.

Church architecture — much of it ancient, all of it beautiful — also attracts visitors. There are still many churches built according to original Roman, Greek, Turkish, and Gothic designs. Many examples of Islamic architecture appear in mosques in southern parts of the country. Italian influence shows in churches constructed during the Renaissance, a period of history extending from the early 14th to late 16th centuries.

The earliest construction still standing is probably Roman. An arena in the northeast city of Pula dates from the first century before Christ. Modern Yugoslavs appreciate such ancient structures as well as the art they continue to create. One of the older art forms, the painting of icons, or religious pictures, continues to be popular in parts of the country. There is also Art Nouveau, a popular kind of painting and sculpture that began about 1900. Finally, naive painting, which seems like the simple work of untrained artists, has become popular enough to have its own school.

Poets, actors, writers, musicians, and other artists supported guerrilla fighters during World War II. But when Tito came to power, his government heavily censored and restricted their work. Since that time, government leaders have tried to keep a rein on artists without wiping out their creativity. A former friend of Tito, Milovan Djilas, has been imprisoned in the past for his writings, which are thought to be anti-communist. Other famous Yugoslav cultural figures include the writer Ivo Andric, who won the Nobel Prize, and Oscar-winning cartoonist Dusan Vukotic.

A painting in the school of Naive Art.

The number of languages in the country hamper the growth of publishing, radio, television, and motion pictures. So do government controls on speech and expression. Even so, the country hosts a film festival each year at the amphitheater at Pula. Ethnic groups remember and preserve their heritage in a variety of ways — more than 100 museums exist in Serbia alone.

Sports and Recreation

Yugoslavs enjoy a wide range of sports. Warm-weather activities include swimming, salt-water and freshwater fishing, boating, hiking, climbing, cycling, and soccer. Soccer, called football, is the most popular sport. People of all ages play it.

Winter sports include skiing and hockey. Sports enjoyed all year include hunting and indoor activities such as gymnastics, basketball, table tennis, and chess. In fact, Yugoslavia ranks just behind the Soviet Union in the number of chess players awarded the title of Grandmaster by the World Chess Federation.

Visiting a spa has a strong sports connection. People who want to remain active treat themselves at one of the country's many spas. A spa is a place where people bathe in special spring water (or mud!) that is sometimes hot and that bubbles out of the earth. Many Europeans believe such baths keep them young or help them recover from stress or illness.

Belgrade: The White City

Belgrade, whose name means "white city" or "white fortress," got its name from the large fortress built high above the two rivers that meet in the city. Actually, the ancient Romans were the first to build a fort in this strategic place. The fortress that stands today was built by the Serbs during the Middle Ages.

When the Turks conquered Serbia, they renamed the city Darol-i-Jihad, or "home of wars for the faith." In addition to the great fortress, called the Kalemegdan, there are still many traces of Turkish rule in modern Belgrade, including a mosque. The Kalemegdan itself has a military museum.

The city became the nation's capital in 1918, and is the home of Yugoslavia's old royal palace. It also has the National Museum and the Museum of Modern Art. Most buildings used by the government, including the premier's house, are in a newer outlying area called New Belgrade.

Nazi troops damaged or destroyed many of Belgrade's older buildings during World War II, but the people have restored a good number of them, including a fine Eastern Orthodox cathedral built in the 1800s. They make an interesting contrast to Belgrade's modern buildings.

Even today, Belgrade's location on two major rivers and its railroad connections make it important. The city's many industries, including heavy machinery, food processing, and textiles, receive and ship goods by boat and train.

Yugoslavs in North America

In many North American cities there are neighborhoods where Yugoslavs have settled and established churches, shops, and restaurants. The Yugoslavs are known for their delicious food, so their restaurants are usually popular.

Recently, the number of Yugoslavs who intend to live in North America permanently has dropped. In 1978, for instance, 927 immigrants to Canada came from Yugoslavia; by 1984, the number had dropped by about 500. In the United States, the number fluctuates from year to year. In 1977 nearly 3,000 Yugoslavs immigrated, but the number has swung from 1,500 to 2,000 since then.

Because of economic problems, some Yugoslavs leave their country to work elsewhere and then return home with their savings. In recent years, 200 to 500 have entered Canada each year seeking temporary work. In the United States, about 30,000 visit each year to vacation, study, or do business.

Glossary of Yugoslav Terms

dinar (DEE-nahr) . . . . Yugoslavian unit of money
dobar dan (DOH-bar dahn) . . . . good day
majka (MAH-EE-kah) . . . . mother
molim vas (MO-leem-vahs) . . . . please
najlepše (NAH-EE-lehp-sheh) . . . . thank you
otac (OH-tahts) . . . . father
prijatelica (PREE-yah-tell-yeh-ee-tsah) . . . . . . friend (female)
prijatelj (PREE-yah-tell-yeh) . . . . friend (male)
salaš (SAH-lahsh) . . . . farm
škole (SHKOH-leh) . . . . school
šljivovicu (SHLYEE-vo-vee-tsoo) . . . . a plum brandy, Yugoslavia's native drink
učitelj (OOH-chee-TEH-lyeh) . . . . teacher

More Books About Yugoslavia

Ancient Civilizations. Millard (Franklin Watts)
Czechs and Slovaks in America. Roucek (Lerner)
Journey from the Past: A History of the Western World. Hauptly (Childrens Press)
Yugoslavia. Greene (Childrens Press)

Things to Do—Research

Yugoslavia has had a stormy history, and the people continue to struggle with the problems of unifying separate groups into one nation. As you read more about this nation so rich with cultural differences, watch for current facts. Two library publications that will help you find recent information are:

Readers' Guide to Periodical Literature
Children's Magazine Guide

For answers to questions about life in Yugoslavia, look up *Yugoslavia* in these two publications. They will send you to recent articles.

1. Learn more about the Yugoslavian ethnic groups mentioned in this book. Find out how their costumes, traditions, religions, and foods differ from group to group.

2. Like many European countries, Yugoslavia has centuries-old architecture standing beside modern structures. Find out more about the buildings that stand in Belgrade, Yugoslavia's capital. What did the city look like before World War II? What buildings remain standing now? What modern buildings have been erected?

3. Yugoslavia has two major Christian sects—Eastern Orthodox and Roman Catholic. The Roman Catholics are primarily in the west; Eastern Orthodox Christians are mainly in the east. Learn more about when and how these sects rose where they did. Have these sect differences caused problems for the people? How are the faiths similar?

4. Imagine yourself as a child living in Yugoslavia. What would your school be like? What sports or cultural activities would you take part in? How would your parents support you? What would you do for entertainment after school and on weekends?

More Things to Do—Activities

These projects are designed to encourage you to think more about Yugoslavia. They offer ideas for projects that you can do at school or at home.

1. Try writing some words using the Cyrillic alphabet. Your library should have a book that shows the forms of these letters.

2. How far is Belgrade from where you live? Using maps, travel guides, travel agents, or any other resources you know of, find out how you could get there and how long it would take.

3. If you would like a pen pal in Yugoslavia, write to these people:

International Pen Friends
P.O. Box 290065
Brooklyn, NY 11229-0001

Worldwide Pen Friends
P.O. Box 6896
Thousand Oaks, CA 91359

Be sure to tell them what country you
want your pen pal to be from. Also
include your age, full name, and address.

Index

Adriatic Sea 6, 24, 25, 27, 34, 41, 49, 53
agriculture 6, 13, 14, 16, 18, 19, 37, 45,
    56, 58
Albania 46, 52, 53, 57, 58
Alexander I 50
Alexander the Great 58
ALPHABETS 44
    Cyrillic 49; English 56;
    Latin 56; Russian 57
Andric, Ivo 59
Archduke Francis Ferdinand 50
architecture 12-27, 46, 58-59
art 53, 58, 59
Austria 47, 49, 53
Austro-Hungarian Empire 47, 49, 50

Bar 58
Belgrade 46, 48, 53, 57, 60
Bosnia-Hercegovina 44, 49, 52, 57, 58
Bulgaria 46, 53

Cavtat 14, 22, 33, 41
Cilipi 6, 8, 15, 16, 20, 24, 28, 33, 43
climate 16, 47, 53
communism (communists) 35, 50, 51,
    52, 57, 59
costume 20, 22, 44, 45, 46, 47, 58
Croatia 45, 49, 52, 57
currency 53
customs 12, 44, 45, 47
Cyril, St. 49

Dalmatian Coast 22, 49, 56, 57, 58
dance 22, 29
dinar 53
Djilas, Milovan 59
Dubrovnik 14, 22, 24, 26, 27, 28, 29, 57

earthquake 27, 46, 58
education (see also schools) 27, 34, 35
ethnic groups 44, 45, 46, 47, 48, 53, 56,
    57, 58, 59
Europe (Europeans) 24, 47, 49, 50 52,
    56, 58

family 10, 14, 44, 51
farmers/farming (see agriculture)
food 11, 14, 18, 19, 20, 28, 29, 31, 35,
    42, 44, 45

Germany 35, 50
government 14, 27, 28, 35, 44, 45, 50,
    51, 52, 53, 56, 57, 59
Greece 46, 49, 53, 58
guerrillas 50, 51, 59
Gypsies 50

Habsburgs 49
health care 27
history 44-51, 53, 58, 59
Hitler, Adolf 50
holidays 20, 41, 42, 43, 58
Hungary 49, 53

Illyria 49
Illyricum 49
independence 28, 50
Italy (Italians) 49, 50, 53, 58

Kalemegdan 46, 60
Kameni Most 46
King Alexander I 50
King Peter I 50
King Peter II 50
King Stephen Dušan 49
Kingdom of the Serbs, Croats, and
    Slovenes 50
Kolo 22, 29
Kosovo 52, 56, 57

Land of the Southern Slavs 50, 57
LANGUAGES 44, 45, 53, 58, 59
    Croatian 34; English 34, 37, 43;
    Macedonian 46, 57; Serbo-Croatian
    56, 57; Slovenian 57
Libertas 27
Lipica 47
Lippizaner horses 47
Ljubljana 58

Macedonia 46, 49, 52, 58
market 29
Medjugorje 57
Methodius, St. 49
missionaries 49
Moesia 49
Montenegro 49, 50, 52, 58
MOUNTAINS 8, 47
    Dinaric Alps 57; Julian Alps 53, 57

Nazis 35, 50, 51
Nobel Prize 59
North America 14, 56

Olympic Games 44, 53, 57

Pannonia 49
partisans 51
Pearl of the Adriatic Sea 24
PEOPLES
    Albanians 56, 57, 58; Austrians 44, 49,
    51; Avars 46; Bosnian Muslims 56;
    Bulgarians 49, 56; Croats 13, 20, 45,
    49, 50, 51, 56, 57; Czechs 56;
    Europeans 60; Germans 46, 47, 49,
    50, 51; Greeks 49, 58; Hungarians 45,
    46, 56; Huns 46; Italians 47, 49, 56,
    58; Jews 50; Macedonians 50, 56;
    Montenegrins 50, 56; Muslims 56, 57;
    Romans 24, 49, 57, 58, 59 ,60;
    Romanians 45, 56; Ruthenes 45, 56;
    Serbo-Croatians 34; Serbs (Serbians)
    20, 34, 49, 50, 56, 57, 60; Slavs 49,
    58; Slovaks 45, 56; Slovenes 50, 56;
    Soviets 51; Turks (Turkish) 44, 45, 47,
    49, 56, 58, 60; Vlach 58; Yugoslavs
    51, 53, 56, 57, 58, 59, 60, 61
Pijaca 29
Placa 26
plague 27
Podgorica 58
pollution 41
population 45, 56
Prince Regent Paul 50

Princip, Gavrilo 44, 50
Pula 59

recreation 59
RELIGION 20, 21, 23, 44
    Eastern Orthodoxy 57, 58, 60; Islam
    46, 57, 58; Roman Catholicism 57
RIVERS
    Danube 46, 53, 57; Sava 46
Romania 53
Rome 27
rural life 15

Sarajevo 44, 50, 53, 57
schools (see also education) 30, 31, 32,
    33, 36, 37, 45, 53
Serbia 46, 49, 50, 52, 56, 57, 58
Serbo-Croatian 34
Skopje 46, 58
slave trade 27
šljivovicu 58
Slovenia 47, 52, 58
socialism (socialists) 35, 48, 51, 52
Soviet Union 51, 52, 59
Spain 27
Switzerland 58

tidal wave 27
Tito, Josip Broz 51
Titograd 58, 59
tourism 14, 24, 26, 28, 29, 37, 56, 57
Turkey 27, 44, 46, 49

United States 13

Venice (Venetians) 45, 49
Vojvodina 45, 52

World Chess Federation 59
World War I 44, 50
World War II 35, 46, 47, 50, 51, 56, 59
Wyoming 53

Zagreb 51, 57